This book is dedicated to captive dolphins everywhere.

Published in the United States in 1998 by The Millbrook Press, Inc. 2 Old New Milford Road, Brookfield, CT 06804

A TEMPLAR BOOK
Devised and produced by The Templar Company plc, Pippbrook Mill, London Road, Dorking, Surrey RH4 1JE,
in association with the Born Free Foundation.

Library of Congress Cataloging-in-Publication Data
McKenna, Virginia, 1931—
Back to the blue / written by Virginia McKenna ; illustrated by Ian Andrew.
p. cm. — (Born free wildlife books)
"A Templar Book."
Summary: Tells the story of three dolphins in captivity in the United Kingdom who are returned to the wild. Includes a section with
facts and photographs about the real rescue effort on which the story was based.
ISBN 0-7613-0409-6 (lib. bdg.)
1. Dolphins—Juvenile fiction. [1. Dolphins—Fiction. 2. Wildlife rescue—Fiction.] I. Andrew, Ian P., 1962- ill. II. Title. III. Series.
PZ10.3.M1935Bac 1988
[Fic]—dc21   97-34229
                                               CIP
                                               AC

Edited by AJ Wood. Designed by Mike Jolley.
This book has been printed and bound in Belgium using 100% recycled paper.
No dioxin-producing chlorine is used in the manufacturing process.

WRITTEN BY *Virginia McKenna*

back to the blue

ILLUSTRATED BY *Ian Andrew*

THE MILLBROOK PRESS
BROOKFIELD, CT

In the 1970s, there were thirty dolphin shows in the United Kingdom. By 1989, there were three. Today there are none.

This is the story of how two such shows were closed, and how their three dolphin captives were given the chance for freedom. It is also a story of many people's help, kindness, and commitment to our campaign. Without their assistance the release of these most remarkable animals would never have been possible.

Virginia McKenna

VIRGINIA MCKENNA
The Born Free Foundation

Back to the Blue

It was very quiet outside the Marineland aquarium: a gray morning, misty and cool. The only sound to be heard was the plaintive cry of the seagulls whirling and swooping over the sea, just a stone's throw away.

It was quiet inside, too. The dolphin show wasn't due to start for hours, and the only movement that would have caught your eye was a silvery-gray shape swimming around and around in the water, occasionally stopping to lift its head above the surface. This was Rocky, Marineland's only dolphin. His friend, Lady, had died a few months earlier and now Rocky spent his life alone in the barren concrete pool that was his home.

It was almost nineteen years since Rocky had been captured from the wild, snatched from his family by men in boats and brought into the world of the dolphin circus. He had been trained to do tricks, to jump through hoops, to touch a ball held high up in the air, to "sing" a song to entertain the crowds.

After such a long time in captivity,
he could only dimly remember the brief
taste of freedom he had when he was young.

Back to the Blue

As Rocky swam around the pool, he noticed a figure standing alone.
It was a figure that he had seen before, a woman who came day after
day and who watched him with eyes that were sad and filled with tears.

What Rocky did not know was that this woman wanted to help him. Her name
was Bev and she knew how dolphins were supposed to live – surrounded by
their families and friends, racing and playing, jumping and diving in the great,
wild, open ocean that was their rightful home. She knew how they communicated
with each other, whistling and squeaking and clicking, and how the echo of
their clicks helped them to identify other objects in the sea – like fish or boats
or people - bouncing back to the dolphins to tell them what lay ahead.

Bev also knew that the water of the aquarium
was not living water, like the sea, filled with plants and fish
and currents and sounds. Instead, Rocky lived in a lifeless world where
the only object he could click off was the side of a concrete pool.

Back to the Blue

Rocky wondered if Bev knew he was lonely. His face always seemed to be smiling because that was the way his jaw was shaped. But Bev knew very well that his look of happiness was an illusion, and she determined then and there to do something about it.

As the days went by, Rocky noticed that more and more people were visiting the pool, and Bev was always with them. He could sense that they were watching him, talking about him, but not in the way that the ordinary visitors did. Sometimes when they talked, their voices were raised, anxious, and excited. Rocky was confused. What were they talking about? Was it something to do with him?

Back to the Blue

Then one day, Rocky found himself being lifted from the water by a group of people. He was taken on a long journey and put into another pool. It was much like his last one – except that it had other dolphins in it.

In the days that followed, Rocky became more and more puzzled. Lots of people came to visit him at the new pool—faces he did not recognize. Sometimes their voices were loud and angry. They seemed to be arguing about him.

Then one night he found himself being lifted from the water for a second time and put in a big sheepskin-lined sling inside a van. He did not know these people either, but they had kind faces.

They stood around him speaking in soothing, comforting voices, touching him with gentle hands. And, although he was frightened, Rocky sensed that in some way these people were trying to help him.

When the van stopped moving, Rocky felt his sling, in its carrying cradle, being raised up and then gently set down again. He seemed to be inside some kind of long tunnel. Around him were the same kind faces he had seen in the van and they were speaking to him in low, friendly voices.

Being in the tunnel made Rocky feel strange. There were all sorts of odd noises that he did not recognize, and once he felt a strange sensation course its way through his entire body. Luckily, the people around him seemed to understand his problems. They never left his side and their constant kindness helped to reassure him. One man in particular kept looking at him with the greatest concern, peering into his eyes and gently stroking his head. Others rubbed his skin with a soothing cream and kept him cool with gentle sprays of water.

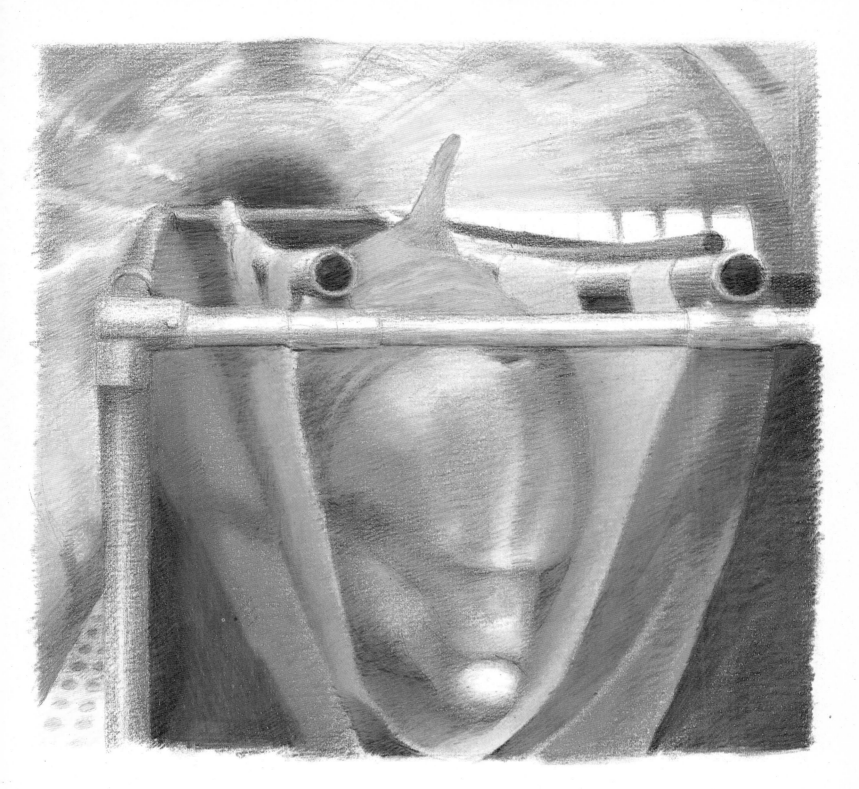

Back to the Blue

Little did Rocky realize
that he was being taken on a journey—
a journey that would change his life.
For ahead of him lay a world that captive
dolphins can only dream of...

Far away, in the West Indies, clear blue waters surround a little island called Providenciales. The sea caresses its pure white beaches and beyond them palm trees and brightly-colored flowers sway in the breeze. And it was here, in this island paradise, that Rocky found himself many hours later. He had no way of knowing that his strange journey had brought him by airplane more than 5,000 miles to this safe haven, an 80-acre lagoon where he could learn to live again as a wild dolphin.

Back to the Blue

As he slipped into the salty water, long-forgotten memories stirred deep within Rocky's consciousness. No longer was he forced to swim around and around in circles. Now he could streak off in a long straight line, as fast as he could ever have wished. He felt so joyful that he squeaked and whistled and clicked excitedly at his smiling rescuers as they threw him great mouthfuls of fish!

Back to the Blue

And so Rocky's
new life in the lagoon began.
How different it was from his old existence!

First of all the water was vibrant with life, fish swam, seaweed waved, currents criss-crossed. For Rocky it was like paradise, but he had a great many things to learn, too. One of the first was how to catch and eat live fish, for all his captive life he had been fed on dead ones. He needed to learn again the ways of the wild and, although it felt like an ocean to Rocky, the lagoon was a perfect training ground – a temporary home where his rescuers could prepare him for his eventual return to the open sea.

Meanwhile, Rocky was just busy enjoying himself. If only he had another dolphin to play with, life would be perfect....

Then one day, Rocky noticed some unusual activity at the edge of the lagoon. To his surprise, two other dolphins were being slipped into the water from their slings! Rocky sped over to see what was happening.

The two new dolphins were called Missie and Silver. Like Rocky, they had been rescued from an aquarium – a sunless, indoor pool in which they had lived for many years. Now, like Rocky, they too had been given the chance for a new life.

The weeks that followed were a time of healing for Missie and Silver. Over time their eyes would once again become bright, their dorsal fins would stand firm and they, too, would learn to catch and eat live fish. After spending two months alone in his sea sanctuary, Rocky had come to know a great deal about life in the ocean. Now he could help his new companions learn too.

Back to the Blue

The three dolphins could not guess that one bright, hot day when they were taken 12 miles out to sea and put in an ocean pen, they were only a step away from real freedom.

Rocky, Missie, and Silver could tell the sea was different here, deeper and darker, colder too. There was a little island nearby, but there were no buildings on it, and the only people they saw were on boats or in the sea swimming around their pen. Several days and nights passed and the familiar faces they had come to know and trust kept reappearing, coming to check them. Rocky sensed a new atmosphere, a feeling of excitement in the air. Something extraordinary was going to happen.

One morning the sky blackened with storm clouds, thunder rolled and rain fell in glistening silver sheets. Rocky noticed that the gate of the ocean pen had been removed. Now nothing stood between him and the open sea.

Back to the Blue

The storm faded into the distance and the sea sparkled in the sun. Rocky looked at the opening, swimming past it again and again, wary and puzzled.

It was about half an hour before he finally went through the gap. He realized that the other dolphins hadn't followed him so he swam in and out a few more times, encouraging them to join him, giving them confidence. The people watching from the boat were laughing and smiling now. Some were crying for joy. When all three dolphins swam clear of the holding pen a great cheer went up.

For the rest of that day and night, the dolphins played around the boat. Then they began to swim farther and farther away. Over the next few days, they returned several times as if to say goodbye and then, at last, they finally swam away into the endless blue of the ocean. Their new life was only just beginning.

Back to the Blue

To all the humble beasts there be,
To all the birds on land and sea
Great Spirit, sweet protection give,
That free and happy they may live.

JOHN GALSWORTHY

From concrete pool to island paradise — the two extremes of Rocky's experience.

The return to the wild of captive animals is always a risky business. Even with the greatest of care, some never make it. For Rocky, Missy, and Silver there was a happy ending. Here's how it happened.

Addendum

THE REAL STORY

"The five R's for dolphins: Rescue, Recuperation, Retirement, Rehabilitation, and Release."

Will Travers, The Born Free Foundation

June 1989

A young woman called Bev Cowley visits Morecambe Marineland, in Lancashire, England. Instead of enjoying her visit, she is distressed by the sight of the solitary dolphin she finds there. His name is Rocky. She discovers that he has been kept in this concrete pool, performing tricks for the crowds for nineteen years and that his former companion, Lady, had continued to perform until her death one month earlier from toxemia. Bev leaves the aquarium determined to end this misery.

August 1989

Bev hands a petition to Morecambe Council, signed by 4,000 people. Daily peaceful picketing has helped attract nationwide support for the campaign. In Bev's speech for the council she concluded, "We firmly believe that if Rocky isn't taken from his existing surroundings and placed in a more humane and natural environment . . . this concrete box which has been his "home" will become his grave." The council decides to withdraw all publicity for Marineland.

November 1989

Bev had contacted us at Zoo Check (part of The Born Free Foundation) to see if we could help. Together with other animal welfare organizations, we set up a rescue project for dolphins called "Into the Blue."

The Into the Blue project is launched at the offices of The Mail on Sunday. with the help of Jacky Pallo, Rula Lenska, Jenny Seagrove, myself, and Claire Francis.

February 1990

A proposal is put forward at the Bellerive Symposium on *Whales and Dolphins in Captivity* in Geneva, Switzerland. They have found a site available for dolphin release, offered by a company called Trade Wind Industries and their

conservation branch known as PRIDE. It is an 80-acre lagoon on the unspoiled island of Providenciales in the Turks and Caicos Islands of the West Indies. It could provide Rocky with a halfway house on his road to freedom—a place where he could recuperate and prepare for life in the wild.

June 1990

Rocky's owner, with local publicity at an end and a new legal requirement to increase the size and depth of the dolphin pool, decides to close down Marineland and give Rocky to Into the Blue.

November 1990

With the support of several other animal charities and dozens of sport, fashion, entertainment, and art celebrities, the Into the Blue project is launched to huge success. A major Sunday newspaper in England, *The Mail on Sunday*, mounts a high-profile appeal, and £100,000 (about $160,000) is raised toward the rescue. Expert vets and a team of experienced dolphin handlers agree to join the project. British Airways Cargo offers free space in a 747 for Rocky and his team. So far, things are going well!

December 1990

The heating at Morecambe Marineland breaks down. Before we can organize repairs, Rocky is secretly removed from the aquarium without his owner's knowledge or ours and taken to another dolphinarium.

Rocky begins his journey. courtesy of British Airways.

In the hold, the team help Rocky keep cool, watched over by vet Richard Kock, second from right.

The Mail on Sunday

Various supporters of the dolphin industry, including Rocky's trainer, are against the release program and want to keep Rocky in captivity. Eventually, after much legal wrangling, a High Court injunction secures his release.

January 1991

Rocky is transported by plane to Providenciales. During his 26-hour journey he is constantly monitored by vet Dr. Richard Kock. Water is sprayed over him and lanolin smoothed onto his skin to protect it and keep it from drying out.
He is eventually released into the lagoon and after five days we are glad to report that he is eating well.

Meanwhile, back in England, another rescue is underway. Lucy Maiden and the Into the Blue team have secured the release of two more dolphins, Missie and Silver, from Brighton Aquarium, in Sussex, England. After three years of campaigning and with the support of the aquarium's new owners, Sea Life Centres, the dolphins have finally been granted their freedom. Between them, they have spent thirty-six years performing for the public in a concrete box. Now they are bound for freedom. After spending a few days in the holding pen for initial health checks, they join Rocky in the sea sanctuary.

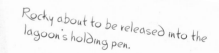

Rocky about to be released into the lagoon's holding pen.

Minutes after, the team lets out a cry of relief — for Bev and Lucy (front row, left and right) it means their campaigns are one step closer to success.

The next morning Rocky explores his temporary home.

the Blue team members. The atmosphere is electric – and not just because of the storm! After the many months of worry and effort, the difficulties and challenges, it is a tremendous release for all of us when Rocky, Missy, and Silver finally swim free of the pen.

Time for a check-up!

Meanwhile, Missy and Silver are being rescued from Brighton Aquarium. Here, Missy about to be lifted from the pool.

September 1991

After another five months in the lagoon, it is decided that the dolphins are ready to be released back into the wild. It is not a decision to be taken lightly since, as with all rehabilitation plans, there is an element of risk. However, after consulting the vets and handlers who have been with the animals since their arrival, it is agreed that it's time to take the final step.

The floating ocean pen is towed to a remote island, 12 miles out to sea. For a few days the dolphins are observed and checked while in the pen.

On the day of release, many people gather anxiously, watching from boats anchored nearby—representatives from the Fisheries Department, journalists from *The Mail on Sunday*, my son Will and myself, Bev, Lucy and other Into

Tension mounts as the ocean pen is prepared for the dolphins' release.

August 1996

Since their release, "our" dolphins have been seen more than thirty times—either alone, in pairs, or all together. Even if we never see them again, we believe that the freedom to race and play and live life as a wild dolphin, even if only for a short time, is surely preferable to years spent in a pool made of concrete, "scented" with chlorine.

The Into the Blue project is now over. There are no more captive dolphins in the United Kingdom. But the story of Rocky, Missy and Silver has become an inspiration to groups all over the world, who campaign for the day when the only place that dolphins live will be in the wild.

Free at last. the ocean beckons and off they go...

Back to the blue!

- There are about eighty known species of whales, dolphins, and porpoises. They all belong to the order of mammals known as cetaceans.

- There are about thirty-two species of dolphin found throughout the world's oceans. Most are gray, blackish or brown above and paler below. Dolphins grow to between 3 and 13 feet in length.

- Most dolphins feed primarily on fish. They are highly sociable creatures, living in groups (sometimes of more than a hundred individuals).

- Dolphins are well-known for their grace, intelligence, playfulness, and friendliness to humans.

- In ancient Greece, dolphins were regarded as sacred and killing one was punishable by death.

- The Greeks recorded many accounts of people being saved from drowning by dolphins, and of strong friendships forming between dolphins and humans. Similar events have been recorded throughout history.

- In the wild, dolphins have been known to live for up to forty years. In captivity, they survive an average of only five years.

- Dolphins find their way around using echo-location. This built-in sonar system gives them information about their surroundings and any nearby objects.

- Each dolphin has its own unique whistle. This acts as a form of identification.

- A dolphin's whistle can give experts—and other dolphins—a good idea of its emotional state. Fellow dolphins will quickly respond to any dolphin showing signs of distress.

- Dolphins will often give support to a sick, injured, or distressed dolphin by positioning their bodies beneath it, carrying it through the water, and raising it to the surface to allow it to breathe.

- Dolphins are air-breathing mammals and need to take in air through the blowhole on the top of their head. They usually return to the surface twice a minute to breathe, but can hold their breath for up to eight minutes while diving.

- Dolphins can dive to depths of 1,600 feet and swim at speeds of up to 22 miles per hour. They sleep just below the surface of the water, sometimes flapping their tail fins to bring them to the surface to breathe.

● The bond between a baby dolphin and its mother is very strong. Babies will suckle for up to eighteen months and will stay with their mothers for three years.

● When a baby dolphin is born, its mother is attended by another dolphin—a "midwife" who stays close by her throughout the birth to give support.

● Not all dolphins have distinctive dorsal fins: some dolphins have a small hump. In other species, such as the Southern Rightwhale Dolphin, the fin is completely absent.

● The term porpoise is often used by some people when referring to any small dolphin. Porpoises actually belong to a different family from dolphins.

● Not all dolphins are found in the oceans, some dolphins live in the rivers of South America and Asia. These are known as river dolphins. Certain oceanic dolphins also enter rivers but their behavior and appearance is very different from that of river dolphins.

● Many river dolphins have very poor eyesight and some are almost blind. These dolphins rely completely on echolocation to "see."

● Many dolphins are trapped and die in drift nets, because they are unable to "see" the huge nets with their echolocation mechanism.

● Just like humans, dolphins and porpoises need to sleep. Some dolphins sleep just below the water surface. Some river dolphins sleep on the riverbed. Unlike humans who do not need to think about breathing, dolphins need to make a conscious decision to breathe, even while sleeping. When dolphins sleep half of their brain is used to rest and the other half is used for maintaining the process of breathing.

● Dolphins do not "smile." What appears to be a smile is in fact an aquadynamic feature that helps the dolphin swim more quickly through water.

● Dolphins do not have saliva. In humans, saliva helps to break food down ready for digestion in the stomach. In dolphins all digestion takes place in the stomach, which consists of three compartments.

● A recording of the clicking sound that a dolphin makes shows it is as loud as a jet engine. It is thought that dolphins may use this clicking to confuse and herd fish together for easier feeding.

If you wish to find out more
about the work of the Born Free Foundation, please
contact us at the address below, or visit our web site.

Born Free Foundation USA
COLDHARBOUR, DORKING, SURREY, UNITED KINGDOM, RH5 6HA
TEL: UK (011 44) 1306 712091/ 713320/ 713431
FAX: UK (0011 44) 1306 713350
WEBSITE: http://web.ukonline.co.uk/bornfree/index.htm
E-MAIL: born.free@ukonline.co.uk